Being Transformed

Being Transformed

*Learning to Understand Biblical Principles
One Day at a Time*

Creola Thomas

RESOURCE *Publications* • Eugene, Oregon

BEING TRANSFORMED
Learning to Understand Biblical Principles One Day at a Time

Copyright © 2014 Creola Thomas. All rights reserved. Except for brief quotations in critical publications or reviews, no part of this book may be reproduced in any manner without prior written permission from the publisher. Write: Permissions, Wipf and Stock Publishers, 199 W. 8th Ave., Suite 3, Eugene, OR 97401.

Resource Publications
An Imprint of Wipf and Stock Publishers
199 W. 8th Ave., Suite 3
Eugene, OR 97401

www.wipfandstock.com

ISBN 13: 978-1-62564-178-6

Manufactured in the U.S.A.

Contents

Acknowledgments vii

Preface ix

Week 1: What We Believe   1

Week 2: Forgiveness   17

Week 3: Prayer   34

Week 4: Walking in Love   45

Week 5: Paying Tithes—Giving to the Lord   57

Week 6: Seeking God's Will for Your Life   70

Week 7: Looking Like a Person of Faith   84

Week 8: Being a Person of Integrity   96

Bonus Days   111

Congratulations!   113

Acknowledgments

This book is dedicated to my Lord and Savior, Jesus Christ, who is the head of my life and the motivation behind all that I do. I also dedicate these pages to my late parents, Pastor Annie and Dempsey Thomas. I will forever be thankful for the legacy of faith they left with me to pass down to my family. I am grateful for my siblings, especially my eight sisters, Jewel, Ann, Christmas, Cordelia, Rowena, Jeanette, Cynthia, and Wanda. All of you have shown me through your actions how to walk out my faith, making me feel blessed to be the youngest of fourteen children. And to my daughter Hannah, the great love of my life—you inspire me to want more, and to do more. Last, but in no way least, I dedicate this book to Dr. Mary and Lyle Dorsett, for it would be far reaching to find more Godly people. Your faith is consistent and pure, and you make all those around you want to dig deeper and strive harder. I shall never forget my Seminary days, when you preached with such passion that the harvest is white and your commission to go. This student has not forgotten your impactful words, and although sometimes it's hard, I will not fail to go.

Preface

Why did I write this book? After studying church growth and seeing many failed urban church plants, I was motivated to develop a program that would lay the foundation for spiritual growth one day at a time. It became clear to me from my experience that one can sit in church, sing church songs, pray lengthy prayers, and still lack knowledge of Scripture. Even worse, one may not know how to apply Scripture. I do not have to point to anyone else in making this observation, because I can use myself as an example. There was a time when I did not really understand my faith. I knew I ought to pray, but why? I knew I ought to love my neighbors, but how? While in seminary, the Lord laid it on my heart to write this devotional. Hopefully, this book will help Christians of all levels of maturity to find practical ways to walk out their faith.

Week 1

What We Believe

Day 1

"For God so loved the world that he gave his one and only Son, that whoever believes in him shall not perish but have eternal life."
(John 3:16)

Recently I was watching a cable television show whose host described Christianity as a faith that believes in a god from space who came down off his throne, impregnated an underage girl, and flew back to heaven to return again soon. I was angered by his description of my Christian faith and wanted to set him straight. But what angers me even more is that many Christians are clueless as to what they really believe and that this television personality's comments really didn't seem to brother them.

In this first chapter, I want to examine what we believe as evangelicals and how we can effectively communicate the message of our faith. Just imagine that your child, who has been taught all the songs about Jesus and has learned many Bible verses, was watching television that night and came across that popular late night host making such statements about Christianity. What would you say to your child? The explanation you would give your child in that moment is the same message the world needs to hear. Everyone with children, and even those without, needs to understand their faith and be able to give a clear, sound profession concerning what they believe about Jesus.

Week 1

Below is a five-question quiz. Be honest—you won't get a grade for this quiz. It's just a tool to help you see where you are in basic Christology.

1. Who is Jesus?

   _____

   _____

   _____

2. How would you describe the Trinity?

   _____

   _____

   _____

3. What is the purpose of the Bible?

   _____

   _____

   _____

4. What really happened in the Garden of Eden, and why is this important to our salvation?

   _____

   _____

   _____

5. Why did Jesus have to die?

_____

_____

_____

Bonus Question: What is hell?

_____

_____

_____

Answers

1. Who is Jesus?

Jesus was born of the Virgin Mary. He grew up, had human desires and human thoughts, and possessed normal human features (John 2:21). He, like us, suffered human weaknesses and limitations. He became hungry (Matt 4:3), thirsty (John 19:28), tired (John 4:6), and sleepy (Matt 4:2). There was only one weakness Jesus was immune to—human frailty. The effects of sin did not mark him: "And in him is not sin" (1 John 3:5). Jesus was tempted to sin (Matt 4:1–11), but because of his divine nature he never yielded (Heb 4:15).

Jesus is God's Son. A pastor friend of mine gave me this helpful example: My friend is his father's son. His father was a husband; recently my friend got married and now he too is a husband. His father is a pastor, and now my friend is also a pastor. His father had children, and now my friend has children as well. His father was a community activist, and now he too is a community activist. He and his father are one in purpose, but each exists independently even though they have never acted independently. Each is a distinct person, but they are one in purpose, in deed, and in nature. So who is Jesus? He is the only begotten Son of God, one in purpose with God, and thus we can say God in the flesh, for God the Father is a spirit.

Week 1

If Jesus was the only begotten Son of God (God with us), did he act like his Father while on this earth?

If Jesus was in fact the only begotten Son of God, did he act like his father? Did his personality have God's qualities and power while on this earth? Have you ever heard the phrase, "If it looks like a duck, quacks like a duck, and walks like a duck, it must be a duck"? Let's see if Scripture supports Jesus' claim of being the only begotten Son of God while he walked this earth by considering what we know to be the three main characteristics of God. After that, let's see if you can answer the question.

First, we know that only God can forgive sins. Did Jesus forgive sins? In Mark 2:1–12, you will find that he did. Why is the forgiveness of sins viewed as a characteristic belonging to God? Well, when we sin, we willingly or unwillingly offend God, which is why it's up to him to forgive us. Yet Jesus also forgave sins while on earth.

Second, we know that God and only God will judge the world. In the Old Testament, the final judgment is described as an eschatological event to be performed by God (Dan 12:1–2, Mal 3:5). Throughout Scripture, Jesus uses passages from the Old Testament to describe his participation in the future judgment (Matt 25:31; John 5:27).

Third, God, from the day of creation, was a God of miracles. While on earth, Jesus demonstrated his divine authority over the natural world by his miracles. According to gospel records, Jesus performed over thirty miracles. These events exhibit supernatural power. In fact, it was often asked, "What matter of man can heal the sick and raise the dead?" as in the case of Jairus' daughter (Mark 5:22–43), the widow's son (Luke 7:11–15), and Lazarus (John 11:1–44). Jesus was in fact a miracle-working God.

From our study of the Bible, it is clear that Jesus in fact embodied the characteristics of God. So, the ultimate answer the question, "Who is Jesus?" is that Jesus is the Son of God, God in the flesh, God with man, Emmanuel, or simply put, our Lord and Savior.

2. How would you describe the Trinity?

Often, people feel that this question makes the Christian faith confusing. We believe in Jesus, but in a God that is triune, who is the

What We Believe

main God? Don't let this confuse you. The Holy Spirit, God, and Jesus all coexist as equal partners. They are one, yet three distinct persons, but they are one in purpose, in deed, and in nature.

GOING DEEPER ...

Your arms are separate from your legs and your head is separate from your foot, but all of them make up your one body. So it is with the Holy Spirit, God, and Jesus. Each has a different function, just as the eye has a different function than the nose even as both are part of your one body. Think of it like this: God the Father is present in Scripture as the sovereign ruler, the omniscient God, and the omnipotent Lord. Jesus the Son is the revealer, the redeemer, and the Messiah. The Holy Spirit is working in us and through us to give us conviction, leadership, and guidance. Together, all three make up the Trinity, which simply means the three ways in which God has revealed himself to humankind.

3. What is the purpose of the Bible?

We believe the Bible has three main purposes:

First, the Bible reveals God to the universe. The Bible helps us to understand who God is and his likes and dislikes. It gives us glimpses inside the mind of an infallible God so that we might know more of him.

Second, the Bible helps us to understand who we are, why we were created, and for what purpose. It is a road map for humanity to find itself inside God's will. Without the Bible, knowingly or unknowingly, humankind would be lost.

Third, the Bible also helps us to understand the past, present, and future. God does not leave us in the dark. He wants us to understand who we are in Jesus Christ. The Bible calls us "chosen, a royal priesthood" (1 Pet 2:9), and if we never read the Bible, we will never know what our inheritance is and how we should live to qualify for such an inheritance. If we don't read the Bible, we also won't know what will happen to those who don't put their trust in Jesus. It's all revealed in the word of God.

Week 1

4. What really happened in the Garden of Eden, and why is this important to our salvation?

The Garden of Eden was a peaceful place created by God to be tended by man. It was a place for God to have fellowship with man. The Garden of Eden was a place of choice. As you will notice, Adam could have chosen good over evil.

Let's look at Genesis 1:7: "So God said, 'Let us make man in our image, in our likeness, and let them rule over the fish of the sea and the birds of the air; over the livestock, over all the earth, and over all the creatures that move along the ground.'" God created man in his own image and called him good. Man was a good creation until he chose not to obey God. This is important to our salvation because humanity's sin separated us from God, our creator. Everything that God creates, he desires to have fellowship with; therefore, humankind needed to be redeemed.

Let's say that you and I robbed a store together. When caught, we both have to stand before a judge. Let's say that before punishment is pronounced, I plead with the judge, "Wait a minute, Your Honor; let me pay for this man's crime." Surely, the judge would refuse and say, "You cannot pay for his crime because you both are guilty and must each serve your own time." That is why when God wanted to redeem humankind, he could not do so with the blood of just anyone because humankind's blood is tainted by Adam's sin. This is why we needed Jesus and why he had to be born of a virgin, with God's Spirit rather than that of a man. The story of the Garden of Eden is important because it helps us understand why we need salvation.

5. Why did Jesus have to die?

Adam's punishment was death. In order for humankind to be redeemed, someone had to suffer that punishment by conquering death. Jesus did that on the cross, so that death would no longer be the fate of humankind. We can live forever, as was promised in the Garden of Eden. Also, it's important to note that the shedding of innocent blood washes away sin or makes amends for it. In the Old Testament, you will find that God often requires the sacrifice of a sheep without blemish, or of doves, which represent purity; it was the blood of these animals that opened the gateway for the forgiveness of sin. Jesus became the last offering, for the shedding of his blood took away our sin and brought us back into fellowship with God, which was God's original intent for humankind.

Some have asked, "How can Christians believe that one man can save the world?" If you find this hard to believe, keep in mind that it took only one man, Adam, to bring death on all humankind. If you can believe this, it's not hard to believe that all it took was one man to bring life back to humankind. This is why Jesus is called the Second Adam.

Bonus Question: What is hell?

Hell is a very serious topic.[1] People have suffered under many illusions about hell. Some people even glorify this place, inviting people to meet them in hell. First, I will tell you what hell is not: Hell is not a place where Satan will reign and throw continuous fire parties for his victims throughout eternity.

There are three different names for hell in the Bible's original text. First is *Tartaros*, found only once in the Bible, in this verse: "God spared not the angels that sinned, but cast them down to hell, and delivered them into chains of darkness, to be reserved for judgment" (2 Pet 2:4). Hell is referred to as *Hades* ten times in the Bible. Hades is not the final destiny of those who die having rejected Christ, but rather seems to be a place of torment where sinners remain until they are resurrected to stand before the great white throne of judgment (Rev 20:13–15). Finally, the name *Geena* or *Gehenna* is used twelve times in the Bible. This refers to the valley of Hinnom, once a place where children were sacrificed to the god Molech (2 Chr 33:1–6). Located outside the south wall of Jerusalem, it was a convenient place for the residents to throw their rubbish, and the dead bodies of animals or criminals were disposed of there. This "city dump" was a place of decomposition and continuous fire, and was used by Jesus to teach about the eventual abode of those who reject him as Savior.

1. Most of the information presented in this section is drawn from Graham, Billy, *The Billy Graham Christian Worker's Handbook: A Topical Guide with Biblical Answers to the Urgent Concerns of Our Day*, edited by Charles G. Ward. Minneapolis, MN: World Wide 1997.

Week 1

Geena is also mentioned as the lake of fire: "Whosoever was not found written in the book of life was cast into the lake of fire" (Rev 20:15). There will be no appeal after sentence is passed at the great white throne of judgment for all who rejected Christ: "The sea gave up the dead which were in it; and death and hell delivered up the dead which were in them, and death and hell were cast into the lake of fire" (Rev 20:13). This is referred to as "the second death."

Thus, hell is basically banishment from the presence of God for deliberately rejecting Jesus Christ as Lord and Savior. It will not be a satanic party by any means, but rather punishment that is inescapable. Satan will not be the ringleader ruling over the kingdom of darkness, but rather will be suffering the same punishment for eternity.

Connecting the Dots

Now that you understand who Jesus is, what would you say to a son, daughter, or neighbor who looks to you for an answer after hearing that Jesus was a space God? In one quick sentence, how would you respond? Share your response below and then with the class.

_____

_____

_____

Now that you have your statement, share it with someone who may not know.

SCRIPTURES TO REVIEW

> 1 Corinthians 8:6
> Ephesians 1:3
> Ephesians 4:6
> James 1:7
> John 1:1
> John 1:14
> John 1:17
> John 4:27
> John 16:13

Day 2

Why Can Only God Forgive Sins?

Let's say you get angry with Ann and say really bad things about her. It gets back to her. Who would you need to ask for forgiveness, Ann or Betty? Only Ann can forgive you for offenses made against her. Likewise, only God can forgive you for your sins. So, when Jesus forgave sins, that act alone equated him with God.

The good thing is that Jesus didn't only forgive sins in biblical times—he still forgives today. All you have to do is ask him. Remember, a sin is something you said or did that contradicts the word of God. Below is a space to confess and ask God for forgiveness.

_____
_____
_____
_____
_____

Day 3

Would You Die for a Lie?

Jesus rose from the dead. There is much evidence that points to the resurrection: the empty tomb, the post-resurrection appearance of Christ, and the origin of the Christian church. However, what gives even more weight to the resurrection of Christ is that all but one of his disciples died horrifying deaths rather than deny his resurrection. My question to you is, "Would you lie in saying your leader had been raised from the grave, and be willing to die knowing it was a lie?" I don't think you would, and neither did his disciples. They had witnessed a risen Jesus, and they were willing to die for their faith in him.

Below, briefly explain what you understand about why Jesus had to die and why this is important to you.

_____
_____
_____
_____
_____
_____

Day 4

What Is the Main Function of the Holy Spirit?

When I was driving long-distance for the first time, one of my older sisters told me, "Keep your eyes on the white stripes; they always guide you right." The Holy Spirit is like those white stripes on the side of the road, always taking you where you need to go. The Holy Spirit is not a mystery, nor a ghost. The Holy Spirit is another equal part of the Godhead. The Bible describes the Holy Spirit as a person, not an impersonal force or influence. When I am unsure of my next move, I ask the Holy Spirit to help me and show me the way, and I have yet to be let down.

If you have a big decision to make, or you're not sure what your next move is, write it in the space below and trust the Holy Spirit to lead and guide you.

_____
_____
_____
_____
_____
_____

Day 5

Why Does Sin Separate Us from God?

Let's say you have only one son, and you teach him all you know about goodness and right. As he grows older, you notice that your son goes out of his way to take the opposite path, which has led to some very bad choices. he won't listen or obey you. You tell him it's not good to hang around certain individuals or take part in certain activities, but he continues to do what he wants. What is going to happen to that relationship? It will become estranged. The more he disobeys you, the further apart you will grow. You know what is best, but he just will not listen. You think, "What have I done to make my son not trust me?" You hurt for him, but until he realizes that you know best and that you are looking out for his best interests, you will remain estranged.

Likewise, sin draws us away from God. He wants to have a relationship with you—it was why you were created. He longs for you and grieves over you but until you repent and get right with him, he will respect your choice. Take a hard look at your life today and at the things you feel you can't ever give up, let go, or get over. Give them to God today so that he can heal and restore you.

_____

_____

_____

_____

_____

Day 6

Why Must We Believe by Faith?

Regardless of what people tell you, when you decide to believe what you choose to believe, it will be a choice made by faith. What we believe, we believe by faith, and without faith, there is no pleasing God. The question posed to you today is, "What will you use your faith to believe?"

Will you believe in God as Muslims view him, without the Holy Spirit or Jesus? That's an opinion, but then you must disclaim the works of Jesus and of the Holy Spirit in the present and the past. Would you rather use your faith to believe that there are many gods, as the Mormons believe, and that you too are a god? If this is the case, why is it that we don't possess supernatural power? If you believe you will evolve into a god, how do you explain that Jesus didn't evolve, but walked this earth as an ever-present God and acted and performed as God while he was on earth? Or would you rather use your faith to believe that God is one God who occasionally uses angels to accomplish his will, and that Jesus is an angel who walked the earth for thirty-three-odd years while he touched, healed, laughed with, and broke bread with people? Angels usually come down to earth on specific assignments, and then they go back. But a thirty-three-year assignment? Well, it never happened before. Not to mention that angels don't have one earthly parent. If you choose to believe this, then why would God call an angel his only begotten son, since we know there are many angels?

Finally, will you believe, as I do, that Adam's sin did not surprise God because he knew Adam would sin—that as he created humankind, he planned to redeem humankind so that he could once again have a relationship with us, and that the blood, death,

Week 1

and resurrection of Jesus created a way for humanity to get back to our Creator? The choice is yours.

Please explain below what you will use your faith to believe.

_____

_____

_____

_____

_____

_____

Day 7

Visualization Exercise:
What Do We Really Get from Our Parents?

Do you look or act like your parents? Some of us do, and some don't, but what we all get from our parents is their blood. I knew of a young lady who had a child by a man who wasn't her husband, but the child looked just like her husband, and for a while the rumors about her younger child not being her husband's subsided. Later on, their divorce led to a blood test, which this lady contested. We all wondered why she would contest the blood test, for surely this was her husband's child. The child and the father looked alike; they had the same features. Later, the woman revealed that she'd known her youngest child was not her husband's because of how he acted—his likes and dislikes, his movements and thought patterns, traits invisible to the naked eye that were in his blood. She was right. As it turned out, that child, who looked just like her husband, didn't have one drop of his blood.

The truth of the matter is that we all inherit traits from our parents, some good and some not so good. This brings us to the reason we why we really should invite Jesus to come into our lives: He purifies our blood.

I once knew a girl who had been raped by her father for fourteen years. When she became a Christian, she began to understand God's forgiveness and realized she had to forgive her father. She talked with him for hours, trying to understand why he did what he did. She felt that if she could just understand why, forgiving him would be easier. During one of these discussions, her father told her that he had been repeatedly beaten as a child and possibly molested by his uncle. The young lady then realized that she had to forgive her father because his behavior had been influenced by

Week 1

his own upbringing. It was as if he had inherited this negative pattern of abuse. The uncle had likely hurt her father because he had been hurt. One generation out of slavery, the uncle had lived an oppressed life and it had spilled over into his interactions with others.

Hurting people hurts others. If she had traced this hurt all the way back, it would have led her to the beginning of evil, when humankind willingly disobeyed God and brought the impulse to turn away from God into the earth.

Picture this. When you accept Jesus as your Lord and Savior, he takes away all traces of your past hurts, failures, and disappointments, and gives you a new name and destiny. Your blood becomes royalty and you become a child of the King.

Explain one thing you know for sure that is in your blood. Write a prayer to God to allow Jesus to come into the lives of your family members and end the curse now.

_____

_____

_____

_____

_____

_____

Week 2

Forgiveness

Day 8

> "I, even I, am he that blotteth out thy transgressions for mine own sake, and will not remember thy sins."
> (Isa 43:25)

I learned forgiveness through a very painful experience in my life. I had a justifiable dislike for my brother. When I was a preteen, I watched my parents work hard to come up with money for a house. It had always been my mother's dream to own a home for our family. My father used his car as a taxi, and my mother sold Avon. When they had saved a considerable amount of money, they applied for a home loan, but no bank would give them a loan because neither had a sustainable income. My brother, a recent college graduate with excellent credit, went in with my parents to buy a duplex house. We noticed early on that my brother would often speak of the building as his home and never give any of the credit for buying the house to my parents. He started putting restrictions on the use of the property. For an example, we couldn't sit on the front porch. As time went on, he got more and more ridiculous with his demands. Eventually, he asked my parents to move out—or rather, he demanded we leave and put us out without returning any of the funds my parents had given him to buy the house.

Week 2

We moved to an apartment. I had a small room, with a closet door that doubled as an exit to and from a hallway. When it was cold, unwelcomed mice found a safe passageway under the heater to my room and made their way into the apartment. It wasn't much, but for a very quiet, somewhat reserved child it was a safe heaven, a place I could be along with my thoughts, paper, and pencil. Although we moved out of that apartment, my heart stayed attached to it for years, for it was the first time I had a room I was proud to call my own. As I grew older, this incident was at times forgotten, but I had not forgiven. My stomach turned at the mention of my brother's name. Still, I eventually grew to forgive him. What helped me through the process was this shocking revelation, a tribute to my parents. I found that my mother and father had forgiven him, for although he was a jerk at the time, he was still their son. A harsher reality hit: He was also still my brother. He was living his life, and I was still hung up on an irreversible incident that had happened years ago. Furthermore, right or wrong, he didn't show any regret for his actions. Could it be that he had asked God to forgive him years ago? I was the one suffering while I was busy judging and waiting for judgment to befall him. As I waited for his day to come, I was not making spiritual progress in my walk with the Lord. I was also held back from my blessing and my ability to clearly hear from God.

Forgiveness was a process. By faith, I spoke the words, "I love and forgive my brother." I prayed for him until I was released of all the bad feelings associated with his name. I didn't see lightening, or hear a voice from on high. One day I woke up and my grudge was gone. I now know for sure that I have forgiven my brother, and it all started with praying for him.

Now let's deal with forgiveness in your own life. You must understand forgiveness if you are going to progress in your faith. So this week, let's deal with forgiveness by taking a quick quiz. Remember, you can't pass or fail this quiz; it just helps show you where you are.

Forgiveness

1. What is forgiveness?

2. How does God view forgiveness?

3. Why is it sometimes difficult to forgive?

4. If you don't forgive, what will happen?

5. If others don't forgive you, how do you forgive yourself?

Week 2

Answers

1. What is forgiveness?

Forgiveness is the process of detaching yourself from all the things that have left bitterness in your life. Whether you hurt someone or someone hurt you, when you choose to forgive, you make a conscious choice to leave that hurt behind. There are three main signs that can be proof of forgiveness: (1) You totally forget what others have done to you or you to them; (2) you disconnect yourself from negative feelings related to the event such that you are not embarrassed to be around the person you offended and don't make those who have offended you feel embarrassed to be around you; and (3) you are able to pray for those who have hurt you, or whom you have hurt, and truly wish the best for them with a pure heart. If you are able to say and do these things with a pure heart, you have forgiven.

2. How does God view forgiveness?

The act of being able to forgive others is one of God's characteristics that he lovingly entrusts to humanity. God does not view forgiveness as an option; it's a requirement. In Colossians 3:13, Paul encourages us to forgive grievances we may have against one another. Forgiveness is a process, and sometimes it does not happen overnight. Understand that our heavenly Father understands your heart. You won't always feel warm inside when you start the process of forgiveness. During the process, you must keep in mind that God does not view forgiveness as optional. That is why he stated, "If you don't forgive men their trespasses, your heavenly Father will not forgive you" (Matt 6:15).

I think I understand why such a strong statement is attached to the act of forgiveness. Forgiveness actually frees us from the bondage of holding a grudge against the person who has offended us. It provides healing and wards off the destructive effects of bitterness. This does not give people a license to hurt you, but it does give you the freedom not to hold onto hurt that could demoralize and deform you.

God's view on forgiveness is simple; he totally blots out our sins, making us whole and spotless. His forgiveness restores us and

Forgiveness

puts us back in good standing with our Creator. When we forgive someone, God expects us to do likewise—to totally blot out the offenses and seek ways to restore the relationship.

3. Why is it sometimes difficult to forgive?

It's easy to say, "I forgive you." At times I have said it and meant it, and I have said it without truly meaning it. It is most difficult to forgive when you have been wronged and you feel that the person should pay you back in some way. It is like being robbed. Anyone who has been robbed wants his or her property restored. When people take things from you, lie to you, or cause you to lose trust in them, you want to get your own back in some way—usually by making the other person pay. The essence of true forgiveness is realizing that you won't get it back, you won't be repaid, and the person doesn't owe you anything. It's hard to accept this loss when you feel you are blameless, but this is the essence of forgiveness. God does not hold blame against us, even when we deserve it. In Romans 8:1, Jesus says to the woman taken in adultery, "Neither do I condemn thee: go, and sin no more." Remember, when we forgive, we can't condemn, punish, or hurt; we must totally release the person to his or her own conscience.

4. If you don't forgive, what will happen?

Truthfully, forgiveness is more for you than for the person who offended you. I don't want people to participate in the act of forgiveness just to be saved from hell. Forgiveness is what God gives you and expects that you offer to others. According to a professor of mine, during Biblical times, if you killed a person unjustifiably, that person would be tied to you for the rest of your life as an old stinking corpse decaying around your neck. When you went to bed, so would the dead man; when you ate, the dead man would be there. It was discovered that having the dead tied to a person this way accelerated the death of the living.

If you don't forgive, it's like having something dead tied to you. Everywhere you turn, it's there and stays there until it eventually kills you. We forgive not only to free the people who offend us, but also to free ourselves. We no longer have to carry the pain of the past on our shoulders; we give it to God and he takes care of the situation. Please understand that Jesus modeled forgiveness on the cross: He asks the Father to forgive us, for we know not what we do (Luke 23:34). Even at the pinnacle of his suffering, Christ forgave his persecutors. As his followers, we are also called to demonstrate this same kind of forgiving love.

5. If others don't forgive you, how do you forgive yourself?

As much as you may love the Lord, you can't make others forgive you. It's your job to ask, and sometimes God will lead you to give back as a way of showing your sincerity to someone you have wronged. This simply means that you will have to make amends. Consider this example. I have two dear family members who both love the Lord. One borrowed money from the other, stating she would repay it during income tax time. As it turned out, she could not repay the money because the state withheld her taxes. She apologized and repaid what she could, but still owed a considerable balance of money. The relationship became estranged. During the holidays, these two relatives would speak and sometimes laugh, but we knew that this relationship was still in need of mending.

The indebted family member began to complain to me, stating she did all she could when she did not get her refund. She felt that she had asked for forgiveness and that was all she could do. I explained to her that she didn't do all she could; she did the least she could. Although she had not gotten what she had expected, she could have arranged to make payments. Besides, she manages to pay a car loan every month. A year or so later, she started making payments on her debt, and their relationship is back on track. I have learned that the reason it's sometimes hard to forgive oneself is because you know you were wrong and that you need to act to make it better, but you refuse to take the necessary steps because you don't want to see yourself in a negative light.

When you have done all you possibly can, admitting that you were wrong, asking for forgiveness, and taking steps to make it right, you have done what's required of you. Then it's time for you to forgive yourself. This is done by admitting what you have done wrong (staying mindful) and professing the forgiveness of God.

When Satan tries to bring up your mistakes, remind him of John 8:36, which reads, "If the Son therefore shall make you free, ye shall be free indeed."

Sometimes the hardest person to forgive is oneself. Remember, God will forgive you as quickly as he forgives others. He does not want you condemning yourself. Remember that he died for your sins. Will you feel forgiven overnight? No, and maybe not for a while—but know that even before the words "Please, Lord, forgive me," fell from your lips, you were forgiven and made whole. That is the truth you must stand on.

Connecting the Dots

As I travel to churches, I am often faced with the question: What will happen to the person who caused the offense? It hit me that one reason why it is so hard to forgive is because we really want the people who hurt us unjustifiably to be hurt in return. We want to see them suffer; we want them to pay for the wrong done to us. Well, someone did—he paid with his life, and that person is Jesus. Jesus died for all of our sins, so list three sins you know Jesus saved you from below

1. _____
2. _____
3. _____

Now, write out a brief note thanking God for saving you, and consider sharing it with the class.

_____
_____
_____

Doesn't it feel good to know that no matter what you've done in life, God has forgiven you? Today, make someone else feel good by simply praying for those who have hurt you and pray that God will allow you to forgive them from your heart.

Week 2

SCRIPTURES TO REVIEW

    John 8:36
    Isaiah 43:25
    Matthew 6:14–15

Day 9

What Is Forgiveness?

Let's suppose that you are a teacher in a religious setting and Sally is your student. One day she approaches you and asks for a simple definition of the word "forgiveness." Write your definition below.

_____

_____

_____

_____

_____

Day 10

How Does God View Forgiveness?

Martin's mother had warned him about playing ball in her room. She kept many valuables there, including a beautiful, priceless music box she inherited from her deceased mother. One day, as Martin was bouncing his ball carelessly through the house, the phone rang. If he had to go back to the kitchen, he might have missed the call, so he ran into his mother's room while bouncing the ball. He grabbed the phone with one hand and tried to catch the ball with the other. Unfortunately, the ball bounced and knocked his mother's music box to the floor, smashing it.

When his mother got home, Martin mustered the courage to tell her that he had broken her music box, and said he would work for as long as it took to pay for it. He asked her to please forgive him.

What should Martin's mother do?

A. Ground him and take away his phone and basketball privileges until the sting of the loss of the music box goes away.

B. Slap his face hard for having a hard head, then get a value for the beloved music box and withhold his allowance until the music box is paid for. Hang up a payment plan to remind him of how much money he owes on the music box.

C. Simply forgive him because it was an accident, but restrict basketball playing to the garage in the future. Acknowledge that he was brave and honest to come and ask forgiveness.

Forgiveness

Which response do you think God would agree with, and why?

_____
_____
_____
_____
_____
_____

Day 11

"This is much too hard for me," muttered James as he walked to his aunt's house. This was the first time in years that James would be dining with his aunt. He hadn't spoken to his cousin since the incident. James had loaned him a set of fishing rods, and the cousin had damaged one of them and then refused to pay for or replace it.

The meal went well, and James felt really good. "Why did this take so long?" he wondered. After he finished dessert, he went in to watch the football game with the guys. He casually leaned over and told his cousin, "Don't worry about the rod; I forgive you."

With an obvious surprised look on his face, the cousin shot back, "Forgive me? What do you have to forgive me for? It's you I should be forgiving."

At a loss for words, James wished he hadn't come. It would be a while before he would see his cousin again, if ever.

Why was this so hard for James?

_____
_____
_____
_____
_____
_____

Day 12

Why Is It So Important That We Seek Forgiveness in Our Lives?

_____
_____
_____
_____
_____
_____

Day 13

Mary was close to her sister Cheryl, and they had always helped each other out in times of need. Cheryl had a brilliant idea that she wanted Mary to invest in. She was convinced they would make a lot of money. Mary had the money, but she said no. It was just too much money to give to Cheryl, not knowing if it would ever come back. Years later, Cheryl's idea turned out to be a real moneymaker, and all her original investors earned millions.

Although Mary is happy for her sister now, she doesn't want to keep hearing about the business. One time, Cheryl offered Mary money when her business was going really well. Mary turned her down flat, feeling insulted. Mary is beginning to think Cheryl is getting a big head over this business, so she has decided to stay away from her.

Who does Mary need to forgive in this case?

_____

_____

_____

_____

_____

If you said that Mary needs to forgive herself, you are right. Sometimes the hardest person to forgive is oneself. Lost opportunities, self-esteem, and finances can make us our own harshest critics, and we don't always know how to forgive ourselves.

Nevertheless, God does not permanently mark us; we can fail and be redeemed. In fact, it is argued that God can make a success out of all our failures—the greater the failures, the greater the success. God makes the bad good, the impossible possible, and the

Forgiveness

unthinkable thinkable. If we have the guts to forgive ourselves, pick up our feet, and keep walking, something is bound to work out for us.

Day 14

Visualization Exercise

Once there was a wealthy man who prided himself on all of his accomplishments. One day, he looked at himself in the mirror. "What a handsome face," he thought, "Oh, how God must love me. There are not a lot of men out there like me, for sure." Thinking he would get no response, he asked God, "Show me my heart, for surely my insides must be beautiful too."

Instantly, the picture in the mirror turned black. The man's heart begun to pound hard, as if it would come right out of his chest. In all this pain, he thought, "If ever there was a good person in this world, surely it would be me! I give generously to the United Way every year and make donations to the children's foster home every Christmas. I have fed the homeless with my own hands. I built a Fortune 500 club with my own hands. What is this pain?"

The pain moved up to his head. As he fell to the floor, images flashed before his eyes. His niece was addicted to drugs. She had once come to him for a job, but he thought she would steal from him, so he gave her enough money for a daily high and dismissed her, never to hear from her again. Then he saw his mother. He could have helped her, but he didn't want to be the only one to step in since he had five brothers and three sisters. He refused to give more than his others siblings, although he had more money than any of them. Countless friends appeared before him—people who helped him in the past, but whom he had turned his back on in their time of need.

Suddenly the pain went away. The pounding in his head stopped. He pulled himself back up, looked in the mirror, and told himself that he must have been dreaming. He had fallen out of bed, that must have been how he got to the floor. He looked at himself in

Forgiveness

the mirror and no longer saw an accomplished, handsome man, but rather a frail, aging man who was all alone. No matter how long or how hard he stared at himself in the mirror from then on, he never again asked God to show him his heart.

Questions for Reflection

Forgiveness is twofold. Sometimes we need to ask forgiveness for the things we have done to others, and sometimes we need to ask forgiveness for the things we fail to do. Today, I charge you to look in the mirror and ask God to judge your heart and remind you of why you should seek forgiveness. Don't take the easy route out of this situation. Even if someone offended you, did you do things that caused that person pain? If so, repent today, so that God can blot out all of your sins and grant you the new start you so badly need.

_____

_____

_____

_____

_____

Week 3

Prayer

Day 15

> "And I will do whatever you ask in my name, so that the Son may bring glory to the father. You may ask me for anything in my name, and I will do it."
> (John 14:13–14)

When I was younger, I was a mama's baby. I always wanted to be around my mother. Whether she was going to church or to the store, if Mama said, "Cre, you wanna go?" I answered, "Yes!" Why? Because I knew she loved me, and I didn't want to be physically separated from that love.

As I grew older, I realized that God also loves me, and that I should seek to be in his presence. The psalmist wrote, "As a deer pants for the water, oh, how my soul longeth after thee" (Ps 42:1). We should long to know God, to hear God, and to be in his presence. One sure way into the presence of God is through prayer.

This quiz is simple. Can you give three descriptions of what prayer is and one reason why we should pray?

1. _____
2. _____
3. _____

Answers

1. Prayer is a cry for help.

In Romans 8:15, Paul says, "For you did not receive the spirit of bondage again to fear, but you received the spirit of adoption by whom we cry out, 'Abba, Father.'" God is there to listen to every cry. He cares about our days and nights, our desires, fears, and frustrations, and he invites us to express ourselves unashamedly in prayer.

2. Prayer is asking.

"Ask, and it will be given to you; seek, and you will find; knock, and it will be opened to you" (Matt 6:33). God wants us to express our needs and desires through prayer. Ask God—he's waiting to hear your request.

3. Prayer is communion.

Prayer is talking to God and having him talk back to us. Only in prayer will we hear the voice of the Lord.

WHY SHOULD WE PRAY?

I can give you many good reasons to pray. We should have communion with God; we should desire to hear from him; we should want to know him better and share our innermost thoughts with him. These are all reasons why we should pray.

However, the most important reason to pray is simple: We should pray because the Bible tells us to pray. In Luke 18:1, Jesus said, "Men ought to pray and not lose heart." Jesus not only strongly advocated that we pray, but was a praying man himself. Before choosing the twelve apostles, he spent all night in prayer: "Now it came to pass in those days that he went out to the mountain to pray, and continued all night in prayer to God. And when it was day, he called his disciples to him and from them, he chose twelve whom he named apostles" (Luke 6:12–13).

Week 3

Connecting the Dots

Luke 11:9–10 reads, "So I say to you: Ask and it will be given to you; seek and you will find; knock and the door will be opened to you. For everyone who asks receives; he who seeks finds, and to him who knocks, the door will be opened."

When we ask, we make our request known, just as we would if we were asking out earthly father for money, or our earthly mother for food. Take time right now to simply ask God for what you want, plain and simple.

_____

_____

_____

When we seek, we look for where we could be helped. For example, if you write a screenplay, you can't submit your script to directly to a movie director, but rather you must look first for an agent or producers to help get your movie made. Similarly, if you want God to do something for you, you must seek out the right place or the right people to help you. List three names or places you plan to seek. God revealed to me that seeking also means research. Don't just talk, but research the information you need, for if you dig deeper you will eventually find. Make a list of three things you are going to research or seek after.

1. _____
2. _____
3. _____

When we knock, we make a loud noise, specifically to alert the right person. How many of us would knowingly knock on strangers' doors if we weren't trying to sell them something? If we know the right place to go and the person we want to see, we will boldly knock on their door. God helped me to understand that when we knock we must have a clear sense that the person whose door we are knocking on can answer our prayers. To knock is to make a loud noise, so don't just sit and wait, but make some noise. Make a list of people you are going to make a request of, and go make some noise and ask. We are making noise with the quality of work we do. What we do should scream excellence. Our work should not have to be second best. Yet we often go unprepared.

I know of a lady who waited two years to go before McDonald's executives to present her plan to promote new products. Finally the big day came, but she didn't have her PowerPoint presentation finished. Her graphic designer was secretly jealous of her and hadn't done his part well enough. Did she really seek? Often we mess up because we are simply not prepared. If nothing else, prepare and pray.

Now with the wisdom and knowledge of prayer, let pray as Jesus prayed for us and for others.

SCRIPTURES TO REVIEW

>John 14:13-14
>John 17:7
>Ephesians 3:12
>Luke 11:9-10
>Matthew 6:9-11 (The Lord's Prayer)

Day 16

I Just Can't Pray.

For most of my formative years, I was a Christian—a practicing, "I really love the Lord" Christian, but I had a problem with prayer. I didn't like it; it made me feel like I was talking to myself. Every time I tried to pray, something came up. I got sleepy, or my mind found something else to think about. As time went on, I realized that pride was the reason I couldn't stay focused in prayer. Do you have a problem with prayer? Consider the sin of pride, for a prideful person can't pray.

Today, I challenge you to pray this simple prayer with me:

Dear God, remove anything and everything from my heart that will hinder my prayer life. In Jesus' name I pray. Amen.

Day 17

A Cry for Help

When we cry out to God, we are in situations from which only God can save us. We are in serious bondage, trapped in a place where we can't see our way out. Drugs can hold us in bondage, but so can pride or lying. Bondage is when a sin continues to reappear and you know you can't overcome it, so you cry out to God to take it away.

Today, the challenge is to cry out to God, for you and for others. When we cry out to God, he shows up swiftly. You may not see him or feel him, but when we cry out, "Abba, Father," he comes quickly. When Jesus was on the cross and cried out to God, he was instantly transformed; it was over. Don't be afraid to cry out to God and tell him what you are going through. Let him know how long you have been battling with this situation and what harm it has caused you, and then watch God move mountains.

Dear God, I cry out to you today because

_____
_____
_____
_____
_____
_____

Day 18

Let's Ask God

Many times, we don't hear from God because we simply don't ask. I remember complaining to God about my suffering and asking why he wouldn't just end it. "You know all, don't you? So you must know what I am going through," I said. Then, a strong rebuke came to me in my spirit, simply stating, "You never asked." God requires you to ask him so that when he does what you ask, you won't credit anyone but him for your answered prayers.

Likewise, I remember asking God for a break on the job one day. The supervisor walked in that day tired and announced, "Look, everyone, take a break today." I shouted, "Thank you, Mr. Jones, thanks!" and then a soft check came to my spirit that told me, "God did that." I was reminded to thank God. When we ask God for things, he expects praise. That is why he instructs us to ask.

Luke 11:9 reads, "Ask, and it shall be given to you; seek, and you will find; knock, and the door will be opened to you." Today, the challenge is to ask God for something in prayer and look for the results.

Dear God, I'm asking

_____

_____

_____

_____

_____

Day 19

Let's Commune Today

In a prayer of communion, we come to God with questions we want him to answer.

There was a man who truly didn't understand his son. He went to God and told him that although he had once been close to his only son, now things were going haywire. The boy wouldn't talk to him and didn't want to hear what he had to say. In prayer, God revealed to the man that the boy was growing up and that most of his friends didn't have father figures, so they always made negative remarks about their fathers. Because the boy had a good relationship with his father, he didn't know how to help his friends understand his reality. It was easier for him to accept their reality and to just be one of the gang. The Lord instructed the father to be patient with the boy and to start inviting his friends over.

Eventually, the son's friends started asking the father for advice and he because a surrogate parent and mentor to some of them. They started to tell his son, "Man, your dad's cool," and the son began to agree. The father could have overreacted, grounded the boy, and pulled him away from his friends. Instead, he validated his son's feelings, encouraged him for being a good boy who made good decisions, and eventually became a role model to other fatherless boys.

This was a God solution. Creative suggestions and advice like this only come through prayer, and that is why we must commune with God.

The challenge today is to look at areas or situations that you truly do not understand, share them with God, and watch him help you creatively solve your problems.

Week 3

Dear God, I don't understand

_____
_____
_____
_____
_____
_____

Day 20

God Said "No" to Me

Can God say "No"? Yes. Will he say "No"? Yes. We may sometimes ask God to do things that he will refuse. We can't view God as a slot machine or as a wishing well. Here is where I find encouragement: God will not do everything I ask of him, but he will always do what's best for me.

A friend of mine was praying for a car and actually got mad at God for not answering her prayer. She asked sarcastically, "Why didn't you give me a car, Lord, since you're supposed to have all the money in the world and houses on many hills?" God simply replied, "Well, I didn't answer your prayer because you don't have a license and you can't afford insurance."

Sometimes, we ask God for something and he flat-out says no—he's just not going to do what we asked of him. Sometimes he will say, "Yes, but not right now," and other times he will say, "Yes," and your prayers will be answered immediately. If you are ever unsure as to what answer you will get from God, here is your measuring rod: the Bible states, "Seek ye first the Kingdom of God, and his righteousness; and all these things shall be added unto you" (Matt 6:33).

What does it mean to you to seek God's kingdom?

_____
_____
_____
_____
_____
_____

Day 21

Prayer Journal

Today you will start a prayer journal. I want you to write down everything you ask of God, date it, and when your prayer is answered, write down the results. Remember, some prayers will get answered right away, other prayers you will have to wait for, and some prayers he will say no to. You can always commune with God and ask him why.

Prayer Request	Date	Results

Week 4

Walking in Love

Day 22

"Greater love has no one than this that one
lay down his life for his friends."
(John 15:13)

The church is not filled with perfect people. Accept this. In fact, when I started the home Bible study in my church, one of the other ministers confided that she had to tell someone, "Creola does not have a halo over her head." It was hilarious to me that anyone would ever see me in that light. During that time I was still struggling with anger and bad language. All it took was someone to cut me off on the road or to overhear a scrap of gossip about myself and I would let the unlucky person have it. There was no telling what I was capable of saying. Of course, God had to draw all of that out of me, for profanity and anger are not reflective of a Christian. Nevertheless, here is what I came to understand about the church. We are renewed, transformed individuals, and from the first day we walk through the doors of the church until the day we are carried out, we will be dealing with spiritual challenges, be they personality disorders, personal struggles, not paying tithes, or whatever else. Christ, for those who will allow him, is always purifying us from something. The one thing that keeps this group of imperfect people together—the glue, so to speak—is that we allow

Week 4

love to cover a multitude of faults. The only way we can successfully do this is to practice walking in love every day of our lives, in and out of the church.

The quiz for this week has four simple questions. Let's see how well you do.

1. What does it mean to walk in love?

_____
_____
_____

2. How do we walk in love?

_____
_____
_____

3. What prevents us from walking in love?

_____
_____
_____

4. Do we have to like everyone in the church?

_____
_____
_____

Answers

1. What does it mean to walk in love?

A good friend of mine once told me, "I'm walking in love, but I just don't know where I'm going." Where do you go when you walk in love? Well, you go where the subject leads you, which is usually to God in prayer. What does it mean to walk in love? It means we don't pass judgment on people. People begin to matter to us because we don't see them for the all they have done wrong, but as God sees them, as souls in need of a savior.

Most of us, even Christians, have the same problem as Cain, who asked God, "Am I my brother's keeper?" (Gen 4:9). To that question, God would say, "Yes—yes, you are. And you are not just his keeper, but also his protector if need be. If he is hungry, you feed him; if he needs shelter, you house him; if he is in jail, you visit him." Christianity in its purest form is simple: You love God and you love people. This means at times putting the needs of others above your own, especially if you are in a disciple's relationship. In order for us to draw others, we have to be willing to give in and take the high road, as to allow others to really not just hear the Christ in us, but to see the Christ in us.

2. How do we walk in love?

When a baby learns to walk, he or she practices by putting one foot in front of the other. Likewise, when you first learn to walk in love, it will be in baby steps. You must start to walk before you run the race. Walking in love is simply putting others' feelings before your own. How do you do it? You stop, think, then speak, and you practice these three steps in all situations, especially volatile ones. At first you must make it a conscious choice, but the more you choose to do it, the more natural it will become, and you will find yourself walking in love.

3. What prevents us from walking in love?

As Christians, we face two major obstacles to walking in love. The first is when someone is displaying behavior that's much like yours used to be. Although you were delivered, you are afraid to go back, so you harden your heart, which makes it impossible to walk in love with that person. For example, people who have quit smoking are often the front-runners in making policies that limit smokers. Is this a good thing? Yes, for the nonsmoking population, but those who have not awakened to the same choices may view it as forcing beliefs on them and may choose to smoke all the more. When your heart is hard toward people, you tend not to understand their position and why they can't escape their condition, so you become judgmental or overly critical, which means you are not walking in love.

The second reason for not walking in love is jealousy. You think someone wants what you have—your position at work, your husband or wife, others' attention—or maybe you want what someone else has. You can't walk in love if you are envious or jealous. Thus, you must search your heart and ask yourself why you can't be kind. When you make a choice to walk in love, all these bad feelings toward people and situations are diminished, and it starts with you stopping, thinking, then choosing to act in love, all while asking yourself, "What would Jesus do?"

4. Do we have to like all the people in the church?

Everyone in the church must love one another, but we might not necessarily like each other's personalities. I tend to shy away from loudmouths. My preference is to be with people who are calm and thoughtful. Contrary to popular belief, not all Christians will be friends. I myself am careful about who I let into my personal space. One reason I do this is because I love hard. I really care for the friends in my inner circle, and when I'm close to someone, I'm easily wounded, which can temporarily shut down my ability to walk in love. I can't allow this to happen, so I'm friendly with everyone but close friends with only a few.

What we must do is look at the big picture, help when we are able, walk in love at all times, and not hinder the growth of others. We will meet people who will keep us on our knees, but that's a good place to be. Just remember to stop, think, and then speak. Memorize that protocol. It's okay to pass on going out to dinner with fellow Christians. Keep this as a rule as well: If you can't stand to be in their presence, pray for them when you are out of their presence. That is the basis of walking in love.

Connecting the Dots

This is a true story. When I was growing up, my uncle R. C. Carter visited from the South every year to preach our Thanksgiving Revival. I learned two very important life lessons from my uncle's sermons. The first was that the more you know about a subject, the closer you are to success. The second was to love the unlovable. I took on this task when I was in grade school. I decided to love the unlovable and see if God would bless my life as my uncle said. I started speaking to a girl in my classroom who everyone hated because of her bad odor and even worse attitude. When I first started speaking to her, she looked at me as if I had lost my mind. I continued to speak to her. Sometimes I was greeted with a rude remark, but I kept striking up conversations. I wanted to see how God would bless my life if I made a conscious choice to love the unlovable. The mother of this same girl who everyone disliked ran the summer youth program. I believe it was probably the result of my kindness to her daughter that my application for a summer job was accepted that year while many of my peers' applications were rejected. Why? All because I decided that I would love someone everyone else hated.

Your challenge this week is to seek out the person you have avoided at work, at school, or at church and speak to him or her. Help the person you dislike the most. Speak a kind word to those who speak unkindly toward you. Put the love that Christ gave you into practice.

Scriptures to Review

John 3:16
1 John 3:1
1 John 4:12
John 15:13

Day 23

I Need to Walk Where?

Mary works with you and takes every opportunity to put you down. She even tells your manager untruths about you. Everyone at the job knows she doesn't like you, and it's becoming personal. They don't pay her much attention, but you are tired of her. You don't speak to her and you avoid her whenever you can. You have never said out loud that you don't like her, but there have been times when you've given her looks that would kill. She knows you don't like her. You have just learned that although the Bible doesn't require you to be best buddies with her, you must walk in love. How can you start to achieve this goal?

A. Keep ignoring her, but start to pray for her.
B. Tell her you don't like her, but now that you are a Christian, you're going to at least try to tolerate her.
C. Pray for her and start to speak to her daily. Just say hello and compliment her when you get the opportunity.

If you chose C, you are right. Start lovingly doing at least the bare minimum, which is to say hello. Pray for ministry opportunities and they will come.

When I was working for Chicago Public Schools (CPS), I really didn't like one of the ladies in the front office, although she also happened to be Christian. She smiled and spoke even when I didn't feel like speaking. Because she was consistent in her cheerfulness, I began to like her. Sure enough, there came a time when I really needed prayer, and guess who prayed for me? I don't know if she prayed for a ministry opportunity with me, but she sure got one. I can attest to the fact that she always walked in love toward me.

Day 24

Do You Remember?

What is the spiritual protocol we told you to remember when walking in love? What did you say? Stop, think, and then speak. Today I want you to practice this, then journal an opportunity you have to really slow down in the spirit, so as not to make a mistake.

_____
_____
_____
_____
_____
_____

Day 25

Can You Handle This?

This is a true story. I know of two people who sit two pews down from each other in church, but on opposite sides. They have attended the same church for over fifteen years. They sing in the same choir, have children close in age, yet they don't speak and don't like each other. They jump at every opportunity they can to take cheap shots at one another.

How can these two people learn to walk in love toward each other?

_____
_____
_____
_____
_____

If you said that they should find a way to express why they so dislike one another and start speaking and even praying for one another, you are right. If you can't love each other in the house of the Lord, you can't love each other anywhere. Maybe they won't be the best of friends, but they should work on this relationship until they are comfortable with speaking politely to each other and praying for each other. If they are to draw others to the church, they must model the love of God that the church represents.

Day 26

What Does "Like" Have to Do with "Love"?

Often we think we have to like the people we love, but this is not true. Look at your own life. Do you have a person in your family that you often dislike, but truly love at the same time? Maybe it's a child, a spouse, or a sibling. Think about things you can do today to express your love for that person, even though you don't always personally like him or her. I have a brother—can't say I like him all that much, but I do love him dearly. He likes to play music, so one day I invited him to emcee a function I was hosting. This was my way to validate the good in him and show that my love for my brother overcomes my dislike of him. I challenge you to do this today. Jot down a way you can you can show your love for a person you don't always like.

_____
_____
_____
_____
_____
_____

Day 27

Is It Getting Difficult Yet?

You have had a week to walk in love, and you may be saying, "Wow, this is harder than I thought." Reflect back on the last four days and think about what's been the hardest for you. Then, in the lines below, pray about it. You can't stop now.

Dear God, help me love

_____
_____
_____
_____
_____
_____

Day 28

Visualization Exercise

Mark really wanted to walk in love with his father, but every time he tried to do good for the man, his father would turn the tables on him and find a way to put him down. For example, he took his father to the grocery store one day, and his father gave him ten dollars for gas. He thought about not taking the money, but if he said no, his father would complain until he took it since he was bent on paying his own way. He gave his father half the money back and brought him lunch that day. Later, his father called his sister and told her what a jerk Mark was because he didn't get the lunch order right. Mark was so tired of getting put down that he decided to stay away from his father altogether.

How would you handle this situation?

_____
_____
_____
_____
_____
_____

Answers

- It's okay to take a break—maybe Mark could pay someone else to help his father until he can heal the scars of his youth and past. God does not want us to be abused.
- Mark could start making quick phone calls for no more than a minute, just to make sure his father is okay, but not long enough to be put down.

Week 4

- At this point, Mark's father probably won't listen to counsel, but he might read a good book on some of the issues he is dealing with.
- It's important that Mark try to communicate with his father, but maybe he could do it through letters or solicit the help of his sister.
- Yes, Mark is still called to love his father, but his struggle should be with finding productive ways to show his love. Mark must also find a way to let his father know how he feels. Saying things like, "Dad, if you yell or put me down, I will have to take a break," is okay. Also, Mark should let his father know that he is praying for him. The fact that he is hard to please is no excuse to give up on him.

Week 5

Paying Tithes—Giving to the Lord

Day 29

"Bring the whole tithe into the storehouse, that there may be food in my house. Test me in this, says the Lord Almighty, and see if I will not throw open the floodgates of heaven and pour out so much blessing that you will not have room enough for it."
(Mal 3:10)

Malachi is of course making reference to priests in this Scripture, thus it can be argued that paying tithes is not a New Testament requirement. First Corinthians 16:2 states, "Upon the first day of the week let every one of you laid by him in store, as God has prospered him." It is clear from this verse that from a Biblical perspective, we Christians ought to be supporting Christ's work and promoting Christ's kingdom works. Ten percent is an excellent starting point, and the more you get the more you should give.

We have problems in the urban church, but none as big as the widespread inability to give to God. This is why most urban churches are struggling, and why, by and large, our communities' needs are not being met. If our children go to private school, we pay for tuition and we understand why we must. We know it is the way that teachers get paid. If we owe taxes, we pay them. Even if we don't understand why we owe taxes, we know that it is a debt that must be

Week 5

settled, so we pay. We pay our rent so that we can continue to live in our homes. We pay our gas and electric bills because we understand that if these bills go unpaid, we won't be able to enjoy those services.

If people would just tithe, pastors could send workers into prisons and shelters and other places in need. If people would tithe and give of their services, the churches could build investment opportunities that would sustain their income. As a way of illustrating God's ecosystem, let's look at the world's ecosystem in simplistic terms. Humans kill chickens in order to survive. Chickens kill worms in order to survive. And when humans die, who eats? You got it—the worms. It's just how the system works. If you take something out or add too much to the ecosystem, things will become unbalanced. Likewise, God has established a spiritual ecosystem, and a major part of this ecosystem is the cycle of giving.

Now I invite you to take a little quiz, just to see how much you know about giving and how the benefits of giving can help you sustain your spiritual life.

1. What is tithing and how much should you give?

_____

_____

_____

2. How many ways can you tithe?

_____

_____

_____

3. Why do some people have a problem with tithing?

_____

_____

_____

4. Do you consider tithing to be a trust issue?

_____

_____

_____

5. What other blessings can you receive if you tithe?

_____

_____

_____

Answers

1. What is tithing and how much should you give?

Scripture helps us understand tithes. Proverbs 3:9–10 reads, "Honor the Lord with thy substance and with the first fruits of all thine increase; so shall thy barns be filled with plenty, and thy presses shall burst out with new wine."

This Scripture helps us understand that tithes honor God. The word "substance" can be understood as "wealth," while "with the first fruits" means God wants his portion to come off the top, and not from whatever you have leftover. If you do this, God promises that your barns will be filled with plenty (in other words, that all your needs will be met). He will provide increase, which is what "the presses shall burst out with new wine" denotes. Therefore, we understand that tithes are the first of what we earn and that they honor God.

I feel that 10 percent is a starting point. This starting point is easily remembered and calculated. My personal rule is that the more I make, the more I give. I'm up to 20 percent, so my giving has doubled. I think it's safe to bank on this fact: Regardless of how much you give, God will always give you more.

To sum up, tithing is giving of your wealth, at least 10 percent or more. It is a way to honor God. So when others ask you why you tithe, say you do it to honor God. When they ask how much you tithe, it's fair to say at least 10 percent of your gross earnings.

2. *How many ways can you tithe?*

I can think of at least three ways we can tithe. The first, of course, is that you can tithe of your finances—giving at least 10 percent of your gross income, as we have already discussed.

You can also tithe of your time. Let's say you are unemployed and can't give to the church financially, but you have time on your hands. Luke 6:38 reads, "Give and it shall be given unto you: good measure, pressed down, and shaken together, and running over, shall men give into your bosom. For with the same measure that ye mete withal it shall be measured to you again." This Scripture does not suggest that we only give of our funds. It simply asks us to give, including our time.

Finally, we can tithe our talent—play free for the church, sing for a homeless shelter, or, as I am doing with this project, write a book whose proceeds go directly to the ministry. I may not make money on this book for five years or more, but I do know that because I have elected to give to the Lord, he will bless me, for we cannot out-give God.

3. *Why do some people have a problem with tithing?*

In my opinion, people will give you two things for free: a hard time and a headache, especially when you're asking for their hard-earned cash. The truth of the matter is that it's not your money. One of my favorite Scriptures, Deuteronomy 8:17-18, tells us, "You may say to yourself, 'my power and the strength of my hands have produced this wealth for me.' But remember the Lord your God, for it is he who gives you the ability to produce wealth, and so confirms his covenant, which he swore to your forefathers as it is today." This Scripture will always deflate a bloated ego. I'm not a good writer in and of myself. All that I have belongs to God, which includes my money and my talent. Some people have a problem accepting this idea, because they like to believe they have earned it all by themselves. It is safe to conclude that if you have a problem with tithing, you likely have a bigger problem with pride.

4. Do you consider tithing to be a trust issue?

This question is debatable, but I strongly believe that tithing is a trust issue. Let's say you worked for me, trusted me, and were well aware of my bank account, and all you had was ten thousand dollars in cash. If I asked you to give me your money and said I would repay you later, would you? You probably would trust me. Why? Because you would know that I had the means to pay it back, and you would trust me to do so. It is the same with God. He can be trusted, and he instructs us to tithe. The more you tithe, the more faith God builds inside of you and the more he blesses you.

5. What other blessings can you receive if you tithe?

When you tithe often, it allows God to move in many areas of your life, not just financially. He may endow you with patience where once you were anxious. Or, because he trusts you, he may grant you a calm spirit that will attract others to you. When we open our pockets, he opens the windows and rains down blessings on our lives.

I knew a person who wanted to get married. She was a "God, give me that husband or else" type of person—but she wasn't a consistent tither. God impressed upon her heart to start giving and tithing regularly. When she obeyed, God began to multiply favors in her life. Her act of giving made her conscious of the needs of others. When she met her husband, he was a giver. She remembered a time when she would have had a problem with that, but now that God had made her a giver as well, it was okay. God simply evened her out with her mate. I know people who started tithing and got promotions, or saw unsaved loved ones get saved, or found the single-mindedness to focus and write. When we tithe, God gives us all good gifts. He only fulfills this promise when we give.

Connecting the Dots

One way we can tithe is by giving of our time. I challenge you this week to take out one hour and help someone. As you help someone else, put those things you are in need of before the Lord. A

Week 5

good example of this is my prayer for patience. I asked the Lord to give me practice to wait on the things I felt he was calling me to. I was later asked to help a choir member who didn't have a ride to church. I hated picking her up because she was always late. When the month ended, I realized that through giving my time this way, I myself had gained more patience. As you help someone else, look for ways the Lord may be blessing you and share them with the class on next week.

Through helping _____,
I have gained _____.

Scriptures to Review

> Proverbs 3:9–10
> Luke 6:38
> Philippians 4:19
> 1 Timothy 6:17–19
> Matthew 6:2–4

Day 30

I Will Pay My Tithe After ...

Katherine had just gotten paid. Remembering her promise to God, she was convinced that she should pay her tithe. She made $1,000 this week, which was really good. She felt this had something to do with her making that vow to pay her tithe. When Katherine cashed her check, she paid $200 to the gas company (got to pay that bill), $150 on her layaway (new dresses for church), and $150 for her insurance, which she had been behind on. She had $500 left, out of which she gave $50 to the church. She felt good because she was paying her tithe.

What do you think Katherine did wrong?

_____
_____
_____
_____
_____

How can she correct this problem next month?

_____
_____
_____
_____
_____

Day 31

You Can't Give if You Don't Have Anything to Give— or Can You?

Larry listens when the pastor preaches on giving, and he always feels like walking out. He thinks the pastor is a little insensitive to his plight. He's married with two kids. Having recently been laid off from work, he is behind on his bills, but he doesn't hear the pastor preaching about that. Although Larry loves and respects his pastor, he feels like the pastor should lay off the people who really can't afford to pay.

How can Larry correct his problem of not being able to pay his tithes financially?

_____
_____
_____
_____
_____

Day 32

Stop It! I've Given Enough Already...

Brenda is a single parent who works three jobs to afford her home, her car, and the nice clothes she wears every Sunday. She has never asked anyone for anything, and she feels good about that fact. As far as paying her tithe, she gives when she wants to and likes supporting missions, but sees no reason to give every week. Besides, she's got too many bills to make that sort of commitment.

What do you think is at the core of Brenda's problem?

_____
_____
_____
_____
_____

We are going to change things up just a little bit. For Thursday, Friday, and Saturday we are going to have an extended visualization exercise that will start with a short story about keeping vows and paying tithes to the Lord.

Day 33

Keeping Your Promise to Yourself and to God

Pastor Hill preached fervently on the matter of Christians paying their tithes. After his sermon, his message stuck with us all, but it actually stunned Mrs. Clarkson. In fact, it struck Mrs. Clarkson so deeply that she thought it was an attack against her personally, and perhaps it was.

God alone knew the vow Mrs. Clarkson had made to God one desperate night exactly six months prior to that day. Things were not going well at the time. She had been laid off from her job, leaving her family in a financial bind. In addition, her son was back from the army and still looking for work. Her daughter and three grandchildren had also just moved back in due to marital problems. That night, she had asked the Lord for a miraculous blessing. If he would only answer her prayer, she promised to pay her tithes and give a special offering to help the church buy a new van.

The Lord never fails. Weeks later, she received a nice check from the government for the death of her husband ten years before. Her husband had died testing gas masks for the army, but the pain of her husband's death had caused her to totally forget the money promised a decade earlier. This money was truly the miracle blessing she was looking for.

What is the first thing Mrs. Clarkson should have done with the money?

_____

_____

_____

_____

_____

Day 34

With this unforeseen blessing, Mrs. Clarkson paid off her house and most of her major bills. But she did not pay her tithe, nor did she bless the church with the special offering she had promised. She rationalized that she had paid more money than most of the members over the years. That thought brought some relief, but it was not the cure.

Months went by, and mysteriously, Mrs. Clarkson found herself using more of that money than she had expected. Now that her house was paid off, it was constantly in need of repair. The electric bill seemed higher. She asked herself why, and then thought of the special offering she had promised the church. "Well," she thought, "with all that money disappearing, I can't afford to keep my promise." This thought brought a little relief, but it certainly did not alleviate her guilt.

How do you predict this story will end?

_____
_____
_____
_____
_____
_____

Day 35

It was not long before most of the money from her husband's settlement had been spent. Mrs. Clarkson tried to figure out what had happened to the money, but no answers came. She had only $500 left in her account. She thought about the offering she had promised, and at that moment, she realized that this money was not hers to keep—that it belonged to the church. She knew that keeping this money would not please God. So, the following Sunday, she paid her special offering and tithe. With the release of that money, she was relieved of all the worrying and restless nights that had been keeping her company for the previous few weeks.

Mrs. Clarkson is now working again and tithing faithfully, and the Lord is truly blessing her walk with him. Now, she realizes that in order to receive, she must give. And if she has to break a promise, she hopes it will never be a promise to God.

1. Have you ever made a vow and broken it? If so, how did it make you feel?

_____

_____

_____

2. When we pay our tithes, what are some other ways God can bless us?

_____

_____

_____

Paying Tithes—Giving to the Lord

3. Do you make excuses when it comes to tithing? If so, why?

_____

_____

_____

Bonus Question: What do you think is the most common vow broken in America?

_____

_____

_____

If you said marriage, you are right.

Week 6

Seeking God's Will for Your Life

Day 36

"Trust in the Lord with all thine heart and lean not unto thine own understanding. In all thy ways acknowledge him, and he shall direct thy paths."
(Prov 3:5–6)

If you are not in accordance with the will of God, are you sinning? To my knowledge, it's not a known sin, but given the choice to live in God's will or not, a wise person would choose to live in God's will.

Many theologians have debated what this means. Although it is not often spoken of, many people flee from God's will because they think it means they must preach, which is not always the case. Being in God's will is simply being the person God created you to be—taking the gifts God planted in you at birth and using them to nourish yourself and bless others. I knew of a lady who had a gift for cooking. She loved cooking and felt most at peace while making a good meal. Yet she worked forty years for the bus company. When she retired, she was so broken that she could no longer cook. Arthritis and back problems kept her from enjoying anything for too long, including lengthy church services. Although she was a Christian, do you think this person lived out God's will for her life? If you said no, I agree.

Seeking God's Will for Your Life

This is an example of one of the saddest scenarios in the church today. Far too many Christians settle for lives outside the will of God in order to survive and get the bills paid. This week, we will look closely at God's will and how we can seek to accomplish as much as we can in our Christian walk with the Lord.

First, let's answer the questions below to see how much you know about living in God's will.

1. When do you know you are in the will of God?

_____

_____

_____

2. Do all people have gifts?

_____

_____

_____

3. Why can it be difficult to do God's will?

_____

_____

_____

4. Are spiritual gifts and natural gifts the same?

_____

_____

_____

5. What is the first thing you should do to start living in the will of God?

_____

_____

_____

Week 6

Answers

1. When do you know you are in the will of God?

First, let's recap. God's will is simply to do what he has created you to do. Here is a simple test to help you understand if you are in the will of God: Does what you do bring joy to others, peace to you, and glory to God? If you answer yes to all three, chances are you are in the will of God.

2. Do all people have gifts?

Every created being has gifts, Christian and non-Christian alike. In fact, the Bible tells us in Romans 11:29, "For God's gifts and his call are irrevocable." Because humanity is created in the image of God, we are gifted, whether we repent or not.

Now, why do you think God gives us these gifts? Let's look at the animal kingdom. In the wild, all animals are blessed with traits that help them to survive. A turtle has a hard protective shell; a tiger has speed and claws; even a rat can hide deep in the earth or find camouflage in the underbrush. Humans are also born with innate gifts, and the purpose of these blessings from God is to help us to survive and make our unique contributions to humankind.

So, does this mean God wants us to follow our talents and passions? Brace yourself—yes. God's will is for you to do what you have been naturally blessed to do. If you are good at sewing, make clothes or work around others who sew. If you sing, whether lead or backup, make your way to the stage, for that is where you will find your greatest joy. I once knew a woman who told me she had no gifts—she enjoyed research, but she didn't consider it a gift because it wasn't creative. I asked her if she realized the kind of patience it takes to concentrate in a quiet place like a research library, and that such focus was a blessing from God. Likewise, what must it take to be on the basketball court and coach a team to victory? When I watch those coaches trying to stay calm on the sidelines in their suits, I think, "What a gift!" I couldn't do it. I don't have what it takes to do that job, but some people are born able to take the pressure, and they actually enjoy the rush, even with a loss. We all have gifts, so we must ask ourselves what those gifts are and pursue them in order to best serve God.

Let me caution that if you aren't sure what you are good at, pray about it and test the waters first. Get an internship. I marvel at all the people who try out for musicals who think they can sing or dance and can't. I know some come on as a joke. But there is always a small percentage of individuals who really believe they could sing for a living. This is where you have to seek the Lord. Don't be afraid to have your gift tested and work at your craft until you hear God telling you to step out into the waters.

3. Why can it be difficult to do God's will?

You have a wife, three kids, and a mortgage, and now you want to sing for a living and risk losing your house? I don't think so. Or maybe you have worked a job for so many years that you can't afford to lose your health benefits. Or, you're all alone and can't do it by yourself. The real problem in all three of these cases is that you must learn to trust God. Do not walk before he leads, and you will know when it is God leading you forward. Will it be easy? Will everything just fall into place? No, but when it gets hard and you can't see your way out, but you are still not ready to throw in the towel—that's God.

When I look at my life, I used to make a pretty penny teaching. I was single, with my own home, the works. Then I was called to start an adult education school for Cabrini-Green residents. I didn't earn a paycheck for years, but I didn't quit. That's God. Some people fear struggle, and others fear failure. If you hold onto these fears, you are failing to trust God. That is why it can be difficult to do God's will. You just have to trust in God.

4. Are spiritual gifts and natural gifts the same?

No, but spiritual and natural gifts can be intertwined. A spiritual gift is a gift that enhances your spirituality and gives spiritual insight. For example, preaching is a spiritual gift. A natural gift is something that enhances you naturally, like sewing. Your natural gift could be cooking, and your spiritual gift could be preaching. Then maybe you would start a shelter to feed people before you nourish them with the Word. There are times when our gifts are not closely related. For example, if your natural gift is golfing when your spiritual gift is singing, what do you do? Sing on a golf course?

Proverbs 18:16 reminds us that "a gift opens the way for the giver, and ushers him into the presence of the great." This gift could be a financial blessing, or a natural or spiritual talent. The key word in this verse to me is "giver." Whatever gift you are blessed with, give it, and the door will open. Some people will make a living through their natural gifts—they might play ball or be good with numbers—and in their spare time use their spiritual gifts, such as sharing the gift of hospitality as an usher in church. Some people will be called to earn a living from their spiritual gifts, such as preaching. Others may use their natural gifts, such as sewing or cooking, in their spare time. I think it's important to note that God wants you to do what you have been gifted to do, and if you follow your passions, you will be in obedience to his will.

5. What is the first thing you should do to start living in the will of God?

Pray. Hear from God to gain insight before you walk this walk, for there will be trying times. I love boxing, and I know that before a lightweight boxer moves to a higher weight class, he's got to get his weight up. You have to get your spiritual weight up by praying. This will allow you to endure hardship as you walk in God's will. For some of you, God's will might call you to leave and move to another city—get your weight up. Make sure you are operating with a clear mind and spirit rather than emotional impulse. Make sure it's his will and not your willingness to do something different. When you feel called in a certain direction and you have sought the Lord through prayer, move boldly. God will not fail you, for it is impossible for him to fail. You can rest assured that when he calls you, he will carry it through to completion.

Connecting the Dots

One key reason most people are miserable in our society is that they are not doing what God has called them to do. While getting my hair styled, I met a beautician who was an excellent debater. When she talked, she had all her points lined up. She naturally anticipated her opponent's argument and rebutted it almost effortlessly. I understood what she was doing because not only was I on the debate team when I was in high school, but I briefly taught debate in high school. After listening to this young lady outdo her opponent in every argument, I jokingly said, "Girl, you missed your calling. You should have been a lawyer or something." She looked at me as if she had seen a ghost and told me that was what she's always wanted to do, but she'd never had the money. I was later able to give her information about a school where she could train to enter the legal profession and get paid as she learned. My stylist eventually left that shop, and I left with her. I don't know if the young beautician took my advice, but I know I planted a seed. We see it everyday, don't we? There are so many people out there who should be in another profession or who need to be encouraged to go back to school.

This week, I challenge you to find just one person you can help, and take the time to point that person in the right direction. Do a little research and help someone in need find answers, for sometimes all a person needs to see is that others see their gifts as well.

Scriptures to Review

Psalm 40:8
Psalm 37:3–5
Psalm 84:11
John 14:15–23

Day 37

I Long for Change, But...

Every day for the last twelve years Mary has gotten up and gone to work at a job she hates. She has to give herself a pep talk to even get out of her car when she arrives at her job. Although she loves the Lord and wants to do his will, she just can't see herself doing anything else. She has been doing this job for over a decade and she is good at it. It's a steady job with good benefits and medical insurance.

As she is driving home from work one day, she hears that the national unemployment rate has gone up 23 percent since last year. She thanks God that she has a job, but that night, she dreads having to wake up and go to her job for yet another day.

What should Mary do?

- A. Just quit her job and collect unemployment.
- B. Take time off her job to look for better opportunities.
- C. Assess where she is in life by reflecting on her gifts, both spiritual and natural, and praying about how she might start moving toward doing what would please God.
- D. Be grateful she has a job and continue to go to work, but request longer vacations.

Answer

There are technically two wills Christians can find themselves in: God's divine will or his permissive will. The goal is to be in God's divine will. The most logical answer is C. Before you make a life-changing move, stop and assess where you are at, then pray concerning where you should be going. I don't feel that Mary should waste another twelve years on that job, but she should make sure to consult God before making her next move.

Day 38

Do We All Have Gifts?

I want you to make a list of the things you enjoy doing and reflect on why you enjoy them. Next, take a moment to look at your list and see if some of these gifts might be a vocation for you. Finally, pray over all of your gifts.

Natural Gifts	Spiritual Gifts

WHAT DO YOU MOST ENJOY?

_____
_____
_____
_____
_____
_____

Seeking God's Will for Your Life

Dear God, in Jesus' name I ask that you bless

_____

_____

_____

_____

_____

_____

Day 39

Help Me Trust You, Lord

Proverbs 3:5 reads: "Trust in the Lord with all your heart and lean not on your own understanding." This simply means that even if you don't understand God's plans, you should make a conscious choice to trust God. Today, I want you to write out some areas in which you will make a choice to trust God. When you write it down, don't take it back—just let God work it out.

Dear God, I'm making a conscious choice to trust you with

_____
_____
_____
_____
_____
_____

Day 40

Can This Actually Be a Gift?

Joan loves her job. She collects tolls on the Illinois highway. She gets paid well, with excellent benefits, and meets new people daily. She enjoys giving directions and saying, "Bless you," to strangers, and sometimes she even gets to pray for folks. When the highway is slow, she gets to listen to her radio and read her Bible. Joan prays that others will walk in the will of God and experience the peace she feels every day.

Is Joan in the will of God? If so, what gift is she operating in—spiritual or natural?

_____
_____
_____
_____
_____

Day 41

The Will of God Is . . . ?

Someone asks you to tell them what you now understand about the will of God. What will you say?

_____
_____
_____
_____
_____
_____

Day 42

Visualization Exercise: The Perfect Day

You have been invited to live in Perfectville. When you wake up tomorrow, your life will be perfect. Describe in full detail what will have changed in your life.

_____
_____
_____
_____
_____
_____

God never promised that we would have perfect lives, but he did promise peace. Pray today that God prepares you for changes. Work to increase your peace so that you can seek his will for your life with boldness and determination.

Week 7

Looking Like a Person of Faith

Day 43

"Therefore, if anyone is in Christ, he is a new creation, the old has gone, the new has come."
(2 Cor 5:17)

In a fast-food restaurant, it is easy to recognize who works at that establishment. If you have ever been in a school environment, especially high school, you can tell students from staff at a glance. When you watch a basketball game, you won't get confused as to whether your team is winning or losing if you know which jersey color to look for. In all of these cases, what people wear and how they look can help us draw conclusions as to who they are. A janitor dresses like a janitor and a businessman dresses like a businessman. It should be natural that a Christian should dress like a believer—but what does that really mean? Take a look at the questions below and see how much you understand about dressing in a Christ-like way.

1. Is it right for women to wear pants in church?

_____

_____

_____

Looking Like a Person of Faith

2. What is the point of church?

_____

_____

_____

3. What types of clothing can cause a distraction?

_____

_____

_____

4. If your clothes are offensive to others, what should you, as a Christian, do?

_____

_____

_____

Answers

1. *Is it right for women to wear pants in church?*

Over the course of history, times have changed. There was a time in history when women and men both wore long robes. In certain parts of the world, this type of clothing is still popular. However, I find no Scripture stating that women should not wear pants. First Timothy 2:9 states, "I also want women to dress modestly, with decency and propriety, not with braided hair or gold or pearls or expensive clothes." When we examine this Scripture closely, we learn that both the Jewish and Hellenistic traditions associated extravagant style with licentiousness. Thus, Timothy is telling us to come to church looking decent, not in revealing or distracting clothes. It may seem as if Timothy is against braids as a hairstyle, but he is not. This statement is an indictment against hairstyles that might be a distraction. Apparently, in the Ephesian church, extravagant clothes, hairstyles, and jewelry were distracting to the worshipers.

Can women wear pants? Yes, but men and women should both make sure that their clothes are decent, not too tight, flashy, or revealing. If what you wear places the attention on you and not on the word of God, it is inappropriate.

2. What is the point of church?

If everyone understood the true reasons for coming to church, many might stay at home. Church is not a gathering place where you come to meet your friends or family members, although it is a place of fellowship. Church is not a place to come and listen to music, although we do praise. Church is not a place where you come to meet a man, although there might be an opportunity for divine connection. We come to church to worship God, to hear from God, and to drink in the wisdom and knowledge of God. We are not focused on other people or their faults; our focus is not even on our own faults. It's simply to worship God and to be in his presence.

I am convinced that people shouldn't look like they are going to a high fashion show when they go to church. You should be comfortable and loose, ready to cry out to God if opportunity arrives, or get on you knees if God leads you in that direction. Maybe an influx of people will attend church on a given Sunday and you will have to stand for most of the service, making your six-inch heels a distraction. In that case, those shoes would be inappropriate for church. What you have on should not limit your ability to worship God in any way. If you are not dressed for worship, why even show up for church at all?

3. What types of clothing can cause a distraction?

Lots of garments can be a distraction, including clothes that are too tight, too short, too long, or too revealing. Hairstyles that are too glitzy or colors that are too loud can be distractions, as can clothing or accessories that are conspicuously expensive. Ask yourself, "Does it matter to God that I'm wearing twelve different colors of eye shadow?" If not, then why do it?

Simplicity is best. Look good, smell good, and most importantly, have a good attitude. We don't have to look alike, but we should all look like we are going to worship God, which means being comfortable and decent. If you get dressed for service with this goal in mind, you can't go wrong.

4. If your clothes are offensive to others, what should you, as a Christian, do?

I'm sure you already know the answer to this one. If your clothes are offensive, yes, change your outfit. If you offend the least of them, you have offended God.

Now, it may seem like I am suggesting that Christians should dress like a plain Jane or a plain James. Not so. I know people in the body of Christ who dress very nicely. If you naturally have good taste, keep up the good work. Is the fit modest? What's loud for me may not be loud for you—I can't wear yellow without turning heads in a bad way. Some people look very nice in high heels, and it wouldn't hurt them to stand or praise in heels. If you're one of those people who could walk a mile in pumps, go ahead and wear them! Let someone show you a color scheme that matches your complexion. God doesn't mind, just so long as it's not offensive or distracting.

I knew of a girl who wore black lipstick, really dark hair, and long black fingernails. She got lots of attention because people were not quite sure what they were looking at. She felt like God didn't care about her self-ordained dress code, so why should they? I can tell you, she was quite distracting and even rebellious, but in time, through prayer, she changed and came to understand that looking that way offended others in the body of Christ.

The more I come to know God, the more I believe this with full conviction: It's not about us, it is about lifting Christ up so that he might draw others to himself. People first come to know us by what we are wearing, so I am simply encouraging you to wear Christ well.

Connecting the Dots

My sister told me of a story of a young lady who really got under her skin. Every time she came to church she wore inappropriate clothes. My sister thought the young lady should have known better. One day, this woman complimented my sister on her nice dress, saying, "Man, I wish I had clothes like that." My sister was taken aback, for she had had totally misjudged this young woman. She wasn't wearing those clothes to be inappropriate—they were all the clothes she had.

My sister gave this lady a few nice dresses. She not only wore them, but because of all the compliments she got on her new appearance, she never went back to the cut-off shorts and open blouses again. Now this is your challenge: Look around your church, job, and within your community to find someone you can bless, not only with charity, but also understanding.

Now we must go about doing with this with caution, for clothes are a personal choice. Just look around you and see if someone has a need you could meet. I shall never forget the time when an usher in my church noticed one of our musicians wearing gym-shoes that were worn and torn. She worked for Nike and took the opportunity to surprise him with a few new pairs of shoes. She didn't approach him directly or comment on his shoes for fear of embarrassing him. She simply saw a need and did what she could to meet it, and a few people were blessed as a result. Therefore, if someone looks like they may be in need of help, see what you can do to change this. Don't criticize the person, but act in love towards the person.

SCRIPTURES TO REVIEW

> Ephesians 2:4–5
> 1 John 3:1
> Romans 12:9–10

Day 44

My Pants or Else

Esther didn't like the new no-pants rule the choir had adopted. She didn't like dresses—she just didn't. She thought her legs were too short for dresses, and if the church leaders wouldn't reverse the new rule, she'd rather just sit down. Why shouldn't she be allowed to stand before the congregation in her tightly fitted blue jeans?

Knowing what you know about dressing in the body of Christ, what would you tell Esther?

_____
_____
_____
_____
_____
_____

Day 45

Why Church?

"Church is boring," Clair thinks. After the choir sings, her mind takes a mental break until the end of the service. What can you tell Clair about the point of church to help her shift her perspective and better understand the true purpose of going to church?

_____
_____
_____
_____
_____
_____

Day 46

My Pink Hair

It took Sara's hairdresser several hours and multiple bottles of dye before she finally got it—her hot pink hair color. As soon as she graced the church pews, people began to point and whisper. It wasn't that the pink looked bad, just that it looked a little out of place. Many of the church's young people hardly heard the message that day because they were all talking and pointing at Sara's pink hair.

After church, Sara couldn't wait to get over to her mentor to ask how she liked her hair. You can imagine the hurt she felt when one of the youth leaders told her it was a little too loud and that maybe she should tone it down.

WHAT DO YOU THINK SARA'S RESPONSE SHOULD BE?

A. "It took me so long to get this look, and they're just jealous," and continue to wear her loud pink hair.

B. Everyone is an individual. It's fine that her youth director didn't like it, but she's keeping her hairstyle.

C. Decide to tone the color down a little so that it's not so distracting.

One would hope she chose C, but it's more than likely that Sara might choose B, as I have seen so many other teenagers do. They keep the hairstyles until other teenagers are tempted to make the same poor choices, and then for the sake of change and sanity, they alter their style to be more becoming to a church setting, but the damage is already done. We must walk in love, especially with teenagers, and yes, we must respect individual choice. But make

Week 7

this a personal note: If you trust your spiritual leaders, it's okay to trust their opinions, even if they don't agree with your newfound identity.

Day 47

I Like It. So What?

You are sexy and you know it—end of story. If people look, it's not your problem. In your heart of hearts, you wear what you wear because you like it, and it's not for attention.

Although this may not be your intent, consider the outcome. What kind of advice could you give a person who acts this way?

_____
_____
_____
_____
_____
_____

Day 48

Cleaning Out My What?

We should always be concerned about what we wear for every day we represent Christ. Look in your closet today and evaluate all of your clothing. Look at everything that you have worn in the past to attract attention and get rid of it. If it's too tight or too short, get rid of it. If it's too loud or out of place for a church setting, get rid of it. If you said to yourself, "I am wearing this for reasons other than worshiping God," get rid of it.

Now, please write down one thing you knew you had to get rid of, and explain why.

_____
_____
_____
_____
_____

Day 49

Visualization Exercise

Picture this. A neighbor you have known for the past five years walks up to you with all sincerity and asks you this one question: "Why do you go to church?"

Write a brief explanation of why you go to church faithfully.

_____
_____
_____
_____
_____

Week 8

Being a Person of Integrity

Day 50

> "He must turn from evil and do good;
> he must seek peace and pursue it."
> (1 Pet 3:11 NIV)

Integrity is what shines through your character, even in the dark. Integrity should direct our choices, words, and deeds even when we not are sitting among our peers in the church pews. Yet integrity is what so many of us lack in the Christian faith. It's a sad but true fact that some Christians use God's forgiveness as a loophole for not doing what is right in hopes that they will not be held accountable for their bad choices.

Unfortunately, this is a true story. I am told of a younger woman who dated and eventually married an older man. Marrying an older man was not the problem. The problem was that he divorced his wife of twenty-five years in order to marry this younger woman. His first wife, still very much in love with her husband, was shocked by this betrayal. This huge moral problem spoke to both the man and the younger woman's integrity, since they were both professing Christians. What's more, the older man was a pastor.

If this wasn't bad enough, I was told another story of a man who married a very beautiful young lady. Early on in their marriage, the couple started having problems. They went to their single

Being a Person of Integrity

pastor for counsel and advice. The pastor eventually encouraged them to get a divorce. Two years later, the pastor married the woman. What's wrong with this story? From a purely romantic point of view, one might say that two church leaders found love. But the question is: Did they seek peace in both situations? How might have their choices been different if they had lived with integrity?

The Bible tells us that David was the apple of God's eye and that he was a great leader. Because he wanted another man's wife, he had Bathsheba's husband, Uriah, killed. Afterwards, David's ministry and influence suffered greatly, problems that lasted until the end of his life. Integrity matters! What we say to people, how we treat people, and what we do to them matters!

Let's play the game, "What should you do?" Please take time to the answer questions below honestly. The quiz is rather special in that all of the questions came from real-life scenarios that cause problems within the body of Christ. How you would respond based on your integrity?

1. You have been in a loveless marriage for almost thirty years. You married your husband because you had gotten pregnant and you needed his support, but you never really loved him. At best, you have gotten used to him. A new man joins the church. The two of you have similar tastes in music and movies. You laugh at the same jokes. In your heart, you know that this man is your spiritual husband. The man you've shared a bed with for all those years was a mistake. Meanwhile, this young man has invited you to an event. You look in the mirror and you see a woman now close to fifty who has never been happy. Yes, you raised two wonderful children, taught Sunday school, and coach girls' volleyball. Maybe it's not such a bad idea to go to this event. You know the man likes you, and you like him. Maybe this is God's way of showing you he really loves you, and that he wants you to feel loved for the first time in your life. What should you do?

_____

_____

_____

Week 8

2. The bank teller gave you $100 more than the amount you requested. You had been $100 dollars short in paying your bills this month. What should you do?

_____

_____

_____

3. You sold a car to your best friend. Two weeks later, the car breaks down and needs major repairs. Should you give her part of her money back off the price of the car? What should you do?

_____

_____

_____

4. You borrowed money from your brother. You promised to pay him back on Friday, but your paycheck is short this week. Should you call your brother and explain the situation, or simply avoid him because you know he wouldn't understand? What should you do?

_____

_____

_____

5. Your pastor asked all members to be at church at 10:30 a.m. Every Sunday, you show up at church thirty minutes late, but at least you are there before the choir sings. Do you need to deal with this attendance requirement differently? What should you do?

_____

_____

_____

Being a Person of Integrity

6. You are a supervisor at your job, and you work with one of the members of your church. You've noticed that this person only shows up late to the shifts you run. You have mentioned this problem to her a couple of times, but she is still tardy to your shifts. Should you write her up? What should you do?

_____

_____

_____

7. Sally hurt your feelings when she said you looked a little plump in that red dress you thought looked so nice. You find that if you look really closely at her hair, you can see the thread of what must be a weave, although you never knew she wore hairpieces. Should you make a comment about her weave? What should you do?

_____

_____

_____

8. Another church leader told a boldfaced lie about you. Although she is aware that you know about her lie, she acts as if it was unimportant. This is taking such a spiritual toll on you that it is becoming difficult for you to be around her. You've thought about going to the pastor, but you don't want to seem petty. It's gotten to the point that you can't stand to hear this woman's voice, and when she prays, you walk out, even though you know this is not right. What should you do?

_____

_____

_____

Week 8

Answers

1. If she wants to keep her integrity, absolutely not! I truly believe that marriage is a sacrament. The Bible really only offers one reason for divorce, and that is adultery, which is almost always an act of extreme selfishness. I am not a marriage counselor, but we must not excuse a lack of integrity for an illusion of happiness. If you are truly unhappy in your marriage, talk about it, tell the husband or wife you have been with for years that you need to work on your marriage and seek professional help. I know that living in God's word will bring you joy, and the joy of the Lord surpasses the feelings of romantic happiness that fluctuate with our emotions. It is wrong to take interest in another person just because you feel you have done God a favor by staying with your spouse. Being unfaithful to your marriage partner invites God's judgment.

2. Integrity demands that you return the money, whether it is to a bank, personal friend, church, or employer. If something does not belong to you, give it back. If it was not given to you, don't take it. We must understand that God will not wrong another person to make things right for you. If you think this way and call it favor, I simply call it foolishness. Once, my sister was $100 dollars short on a bill. Later, one of her business contacts mistakenly overpaid her an extra $100. Since it was the exact amount needed to pay off her bills, she claimed that this was God's way of favoring her. Sometimes, we over-spiritualize things to make ourselves feel better. I will tell you what I told my sister. Being overpaid was a mistake, plain and simple. Give the money back and continue to look to God for your blessings. I don't care if it's from a bank, fast-food restaurant, department store, family member, or friend—if you ever come across money or anything else that doesn't belong to you, give it back and keep your integrity.

3. Integrity would oblige you to either return your friend's money or share the bill for fixing the car. Although you may not be legally

obligated to pay for repairs, having sold the car under the "as is" law, integrity demands that you do what you can to make it right.

If you were aware that the car had a problem and you did not disclose it before selling the car, the moral thing to do would be to either refund some of the money to help with repairs or to allow your friend to return the car for her money back. To do otherwise would show a lack of integrity. You should not seek to take advantage of another by getting good money for a lemon.

4. When you borrow money and can't pay it back, the worst thing to do is avoid the situation. It's so easy to avoid the problem or stall for time by letting the bill collector's calls go to voicemail, but this is wrong and demonstrates a real lack of integrity. I have learned its better to talk to people. If you don't have the money, just say so, for in many situations avoiding problems creates more problems.

5. I never understand why, as people of faith, we often feel it's okay to show up late for appointments, church service, and even work. I understand that sometimes tardiness can't be avoided, but to make it a habit to show up late shows a blatant disrespect for leadership and a lack of integrity to one's word. I truly believe that as Christians, we should try to be fifteen minutes early to events, work, and especially church. Your integrity should prompt you to get an alarm clock, go to sleep earlier, or plan your day the night before. We shouldn't want to be known as people who don't follow leadership; it should upset the Christ inside of us to be labeled as such.

6. After the agreed-upon number of warnings, it would be appropriate and a matter of integrity to write this coworker up. This is not only because such disciplinary action is company policy, but also because your coworker needs to address the consequences of her actions. Favoritism in the workplace is a major cause of division. It is what Satan uses to divide and eventually conquer relationships in the church, at school, and on our jobs. The secular world should not have to fear unfairness when a Christian in is charge. As leaders,

Week 8

Christians should always strive to be just, for this is a characteristic of our Heavenly Father.

7. When your feelings are hurt, your integrity should quickly lead you to acknowledge this hurt. Even if it's a little uncomfortable, say, "I thought I looked good today, so your comment really hurt my feelings." Hopefully, a sincere "I'm sorry" will follow. If no apology or exclamation is offered, you must learn to move on. When you have told others how you feel and spoken your piece, as the saints say, let it be. Learning this forbearance will help you so much in your spiritual walk. You can't control what people think or say, but you can control how you allow it to affect you. While you may not be able to judge the motive behind that statement, you must call upon your own integrity to forgive the other person. Then let God do the rest. Trying to retaliate will not only damage your integrity, but also earn you an enemy. Think about this: Would retaliation help the situation at all? At best, it would only help you feel temporarily better at the expense of the other person.

8. Integrity would lead you to go to the pastor, especially if you're having difficulty with another church member. There is no greater corruption of integrity than telling lies. When we do not act to resolve problems, we also lack integrity. When people hurt you, deal with the issue immediately. You don't have to be a spiritual giant all the time, and no, you won't lose your ticket to heaven. In fact, you can't lose your ticket to heaven, because Jesus paid for it already with his blood. Here is the main reason that we can't allow people to tell lies in church and get away with it. We have to love them in spite of their flaws and have an open desire to see them grow. We can pray about it, and of course walk in love, but if such actions can be prevented, integrity calls us to work to correct the situation. Feel blessed that these lies came to your attention. This means that God has chosen you to deal with them. When this situation happened to me, I learned to see it as an opportunity to help someone else grow. Just like I schedule a preaching engagement, I needed to set aside a time to meet, talk, and pray with my fellow sister in the Lord.

Being a Person of Integrity

She needed to know that I am approachable, while I needed to be a woman of God with a word that meant something when I wasn't in the pulpit.

Connecting the Dots

IT'S TIME TO CHOOSE AN ACCOUNTABILITY PARTNER, SOMEONE WHO WILL PRAY YOU THROUGH ISSUES YOU ARE STRUGGLING WITH.

Take your spiritual temperature. In what area in your life are you lacking integrity? Are you showing up late for church every Sunday, cheating on your taxes, or lying to friends? Maybe you are an upright person, but you know of people who are not and you are afraid to say so. Think of three things you can do to become a person of integrity and write them down (if you don't have three, just list whatever area the Lord impresses on your heart). Then immediately call a prayer partner or trusted friend. Confess your weakness and ask them to hold you more accountable in these selected areas of integrity. After making your list, put it in an envelope, and mail it to your partner. After six months, evaluate your progress. If things have not gotten better, do not give up. You might want to seek out a new accountability partner. If you have improved, use this as a testimony and share it with someone else.

My three areas to act with integrity are:

1. _____

2. _____

3. _____

I am accountable to _____

Week 8

SCRIPTURES TO REVIEW

    Exodus 20:15
    Exodus 22:3
    Leviticus 19:10–12
    Ephesians 4:26
    Ephesians 5:18

Day 51

She Is Just Not That into Him.

A certain young woman has been with her boyfriend for three years now. She knows he cares for her, her family, and her church. Everyone had always matched them together, even before they were a couple, but the girl's heart is just not in it. She hates to say anything, since her mother is forever reminding her that a good man is hard to find. She believes he truly is a good man, but she really wants to travel instead of settling down.

WHAT SHOULD SHE DO?

1. Continue with the pretense, one day she will come to love him.
2. Have her mother break the news that it's over.
3. Break the news to him on Facebook to avoid any messy emotional fallout.
4. Bring in a mentor or pastor and pray over this matter together, speaking about her feelings honestly.
5. Marry him. If it doesn't work out, get a divorce.

Answer

If you chose to talk it over, you are on the right path. Remember that a person of integrity is an honest person.

Day 52

Pay What?

Ron has $100 dollars, enough to pay the cell phone bill, but he owes his brother $75. The phone rings, and Ron notices it is his brother calling. He feels in his heart that his brother could wait a little longer. He has a job that pays way more money than Ron makes. The phone continues to ring steadily as Ron contemplates answering. Finally, it goes to voicemail. Good, Ron thought, he can wait another two weeks. He quickly heads to the cell phone store.

Consider the tactic Ron used and explain why it is wrong.

_____
_____
_____
_____
_____
_____

Day 53

Taxes

Taxes are due. Jim offered to do your taxes again this year. He is excited because he has learned of more crooked ways to get you back a bigger tax return. "Don't worry," he assures you, "it's the government and they rob everyone anyway." What can you say to Jim that will reflect your integrity?

_____
_____
_____
_____
_____

Day 54

What to Do?

Your best friend recently split with her husband. Now that your friend has moved out of town, you wonder if you'll continue being friends. Meanwhile, her ex is now single, looking good, and looking at you! You always thought he was kind of cute, and wow, here he comes. He asks for your number. What should you do?

_____
_____
_____
_____
_____

Day 55

Church Again?

Your pastor reminds everyone to come to church on time. But Sunday is your only day off from work. When the pastor approached you about your absence at church one Sunday, you explained to him that you have been under the weather these last few weeks but will try to do better. As you say the words, you catch a sharp glance from your wife because she knows you just lied. What do you expect she will do?

1. Keep her mouth shut since it is none of her business.
2. Tell him she has been sick too. Why not throw in the children too and say the whole family has been ill?
3. She should just walk away and keep quiet.
4. She should correct you in front of the pastor.
5. She should wait to discuss the matter with you at home, and the both of you should confess the truth to your pastor.

Answer

The fifth answer is best, for although the husband needs to be corrected, his wife should avoid an aggressive confrontation. This is not a matter she should walk away from, but she should use discernment when discussing this issue and not embarrass her husband in public.

Day 56

Everyone was told to wear white for Women's Day at church, and here come Katie Mae in that loud green. She looks ridiculous in that outfit. You really should tell her so, since it would be such a shame for her to wear that outfit again. You believe that you ought to speak your mind. Should you say something to her? If so, what should you say?

_____
_____
_____
_____
_____

Bonus Days

You have successfully completed your eight weeks, having transformed yourself over fifty-six days. I have enclosed two extra bonus days, ending with a day of prayer, and I invite you to reflect on ways you have been transformed. I encourage and challenge you to go through this book with someone else to help others share in your transformed faith.

Day 57

As soon as you brought home the computer you brought from Bob, it locked up. When you had it looked at, the technician told you the hard drive in the computer was no good. You really needed a working computer for your schoolwork. When you approached Bob to explain the situation to him, he said the computer was working just fine when he gave it to you. The both of you had even turned it on and printed a document. Since both of you are believers, what Scripture can you point him to? Based on your review of Scripture, how can you work to resolve the situation?

_____
_____
_____
_____
_____

Day 58

Dude, Pay Me

You have not spoken to your brother for years because he didn't pay back a large loan you made to him, although both of you are Christians. Now he has asked you to be his best man at his wedding. He has been talking up his big plans for an expensive honeymoon. He is your brother and you love him, but this is getting to be too much for you to bear. What should you say to your brother?

1. I don't want to rain on your parade, but have you forgotten about the money you owe me?
2. I can't be in your wedding. I think the lady you are marrying is too good for you, and I can't witness a lie.
3. Read to him Scriptures about paying back what he owes.
4. Have his pastor sit him down to tell him he owes too much money to afford such an extravagant honeymoon.
5. Be honest and remind him of the loan to see if the two of you can come up with a plan to repay the money.

Answer

It's always better to be honest, even before you take the problem to your pastor. I always say that pastors are the intervention plan—when it comes to family, the first and best solution is to communicate with each other. Therefore, the fifth option is the best first step on the way to a solution.

Congratulations!

You have successfully completed the booklet. Below is a prayer, and I invite you to pray for the next seven days as a way of strengthening your commitment to the Lord through the next week and for the rest of your faith journey.

Dear Lord,

I pray that I will forever thirst after a relationship with you. I understand that you gave your son freely to die on the Cross, and for this I thank you. I understand that he is our divine savior, and today and every day, let me trust in him. I pray that forgiveness will stick to me like glue. When someone hurts me, give me the wisdom and knowledge to forgive, and when I hurt others, let me ask for forgiveness. Lord, let prayer become my daily communication with you, let me always remember to pray for my nation, my family, my friends, and finally, myself. As I walk Lord, keep me in remembrance that there is no closer walk with you than the walk we take in love. Help me to love, and care for my sisters and brothers in Christ, not through my words only, but also through my actions. Help me to always take the high road, to live a humble life before you and others. Lord, never let me forget that before I pay others, I will pay you. Help me to tithe of my time as well as my finances. In all things Lord, let me be blessed to seek your will for my life. When I fall astray or go down a dead-end street, have mercy on me Lord, and give me spiritual insight to find the right path. Help me always be in remembrance that it's not what I do in the world that makes much difference, for its only the things I do for Christ that will last. As I look in the mirror, let my actions, clothes, words, and thoughts become a reflection of Christ. I want to not only look like a person of faith, but I want to live my faith with integrity in Christ. I pray that I become a person

Week 8

of integrity. Even when it hurts and my choices seem all wrong, I would rather be wrong in the eyes of others and right in your sight. In my personal life and relationships, and in my professional and business dealings, let me be always a person of Christ.

www.ingramcontent.com/pod-product-compliance
Lightning Source LLC
Chambersburg PA
CBHW070500090426
42735CB00012B/2628